ROYAL PALACES

For as long as there have been kings and queens in Britain, there have
been magnificent royal palaces to house them, and today many of
these survive as national treasures – glorious monuments to the
long and fascinating history of a sovereign state.

From the Palace of Westminster, founded in the 11th century by
the saintly Edward the Confessor, to Buckingham Palace, the London
residence of the present Sovereign, Her Majesty Queen Elizabeth II,
these resplendent buildings reflect both the progress of the royal line
and the powerful and often flamboyant personalities of the
many kings and queens who occupied them.

P

THE PALACE OF WESTMINSTER

THE PALACE OF WESTMINSTER was the first of four royal homes to be created in the City of Westminster, the administrative heart of London. It was followed in later centuries by Whitehall Palace, St James's Palace and Buckingham Palace.

The founder of the Palace of Westminster was the last Saxon king, Edward the Confessor, and the site Thorneye, the 'Isle of Thorns', a thicket-grown island in the marshes on the north bank of the Thames, where there was a small monastery dedicated to St Peter. Here, 'because of his love for the Prince of the Apostles', the pious Edward founded Westminster Abbey, and built his palace on the riverbank. William the Conqueror's son, William Rufus, added Westminster Hall; Henry III extended the 'private palace' to include the fabled Painted Chamber and other Gothic rooms, and Westminster remained the sovereign residence until Henry VIII abandoned it in favour of Whitehall. From the middle of the 16th century it became the Houses of Parliament – home of the Lords and Commons.

Most of the old medieval palace was destroyed by fire on the night of 16 October 1834, when some loads of notched tally sticks, preserved as forms of account in the Exchequer tally room, were taken to the House of Lords to be burned in its furnace, and generated such intense heat that the building was set alight. Today, all that remains is Westminster Hall, the 13th-century undercroft of St Stephen's Chapel and, across the road, the Jewel Tower built by Edward III.

The palace was rebuilt in 1840–60 by Sir Charles Barry and adorned with elaborate Gothic ornamentation by Augustus Pugin. Barry's outstanding landmarks are the Clock Tower at one end of the long line of buildings, and the Victoria Tower at the other. The clock tower, with its four clock faces, is familiarly – and very fondly – known as 'Big Ben', although Big Ben is in fact the name of the hour bell, cast at the Whitechapel Foundry and named after Sir Benjamin Hall, who was First Commissioner of Works when it was hung in 1859. The Victoria Tower is the repository for parliamentary records and beneath it is the Sovereign's Entrance, used by Her Majesty The Queen at the State Opening of Parliament, one of London's most spectacular annual pageants.

LEFT: *The 13th-century Chapel of St Mary Undercroft is all that remains of St Stephen's Chapel, built by Edward I. The undercroft survived the fire of 1834 and was restored in the 1860s with vibrant decoration.*

RIGHT: *Westminster Hall, the great hall of the medieval palace, was built by William II, and was unique among English royal palaces for its role as both the king's residence and the centre of royal government.*

Great Occasions

Historic Westminster Hall has witnessed the trial of Charles I, the coronation banquets of all the sovereigns from Edward the Confessor to George IV, and the lying-in-state of George VI, Sir Winston Churchill and, in 2002, Her Majesty Queen Elizabeth The Queen Mother. The hall was saved from destruction by an epic united effort, led by the Chief Superintendent of the London Fire Service and Colonel Elliott, a Member of Parliament, when German bombs fell on the palace on the night of 10 May 1941.

THE TOWER OF LONDON

WHEN EDWARD THE CONFESSOR DIED, he left no direct heir, but had promised the throne to both Harold Godwineson, the powerful son of a Saxon earl, and William of Normandy in France. Harold was crowned king in January 1066, but William was already preparing to challenge Harold's right of succession. The outcome was decided at the famous Battle of Hastings in October 1066. William's success earned him the title 'the Conqueror'; he was crowned on Christmas Day, and from this point English history, and the face of the English landscape, underwent dramatic changes.

One of William's first tasks was to erect fortifications around the country against any potential opposition. In south-east London, immediately within the Roman city wall, he built what came to be known as the Tower of London, to deter 'the vast and fierce populace'. The White Tower, built from 1081 to 1097, gave the fortress its name. This three-storeyed 'palace keep', built in Caen stone over a vaulted basement, still dominates its surroundings by the River Thames. Its stone chambers and beautiful little tunnel-vaulted Chapel of St John the Evangelist, now a Chapel Royal, illustrate the lifestyle of the early medieval kings.

The White Tower owes its name to Henry III, who had the outside whitewashed in about 1240. Henry added other royal apartments to the fortress, graced with marble columns and wall paintings; he also enlarged and adorned the 12th-century Chapel Royal of St Peter ad Vincula – used as a place of worship for the community within the Tower – and began to lay out the concentric fortress of today, an enlargement completed by his son, Edward I.

RIGHT: *The White Tower, a sturdy and enduring symbol of the Norman Conquest in 1066, one of the most significant events in English history. The tower is built on the foundations of William the Conqueror's original keep.*

ABOVE: *The beautiful King's 'Aula', or private hall, in St Thomas's Tower, built by Edward I. The hall has been restored to illustrate its appearance in the 13th century, when Edward used it for dining and entertaining.*

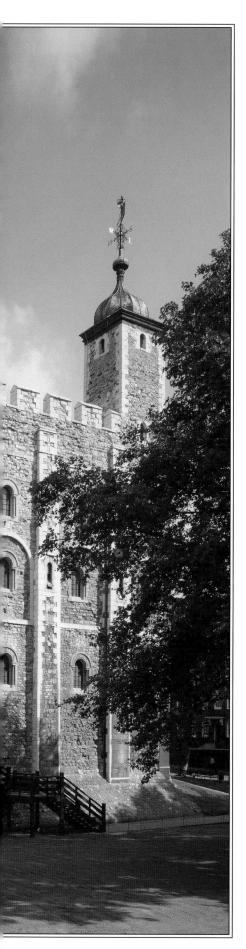

In 1377, the young Richard II rode out on the eve of his coronation in dazzling procession from this handsome palace and fortress through a bedecked city to Westminster, setting a precedent that was followed for almost 300 years. Charles II was the last sovereign to observe the custom, in 1661. By then, the Tower had become outdated as a royal residence. Henry VII's queen, Elizabeth of York, had died there in childbirth in 1503, but the Tudors and Stuarts found it increasingly unequal to their domestic standards.

Today, the Tower's ancient prestige as England's citadel is acknowledged each night at 10 o'clock during the Ceremony of the Keys, when the gates are locked according to historic tradition.

ABOVE: *Many of the Tower's more distinguished prisoners were held in the timber-framed Queen's House, including Henry VIII's unfortunate second wife, Anne Boleyn. The house gained its name in the reign of Queen Victoria.*

BELOW: *This block and axe were used for the execution of Simon Fraser, Lord Lovat, for his part in the 1745 Jacobite uprising against the monarch.*

Prisoners in the Tower

In 1100 the Tower of London received its first state prisoner, Ranulf Flambard, Bishop of Durham, who was incarcerated for extortion. He was the first in a long line of unfortunates, and one of the few who ever escaped. Most enemies of the Crown were beheaded on Tower Hill, although a select few, including two of Henry VIII's queens – Anne Boleyn and Katherine Howard – and the 'nine-days queen', Lady Jane Grey, met their fate on the green outside the Chapel Royal of St Peter ad Vincula. The last prisoner to be beheaded on Tower Hill – and indeed in England – was Simon Fraser, Lord Lovat. The last person to be sent to the Tower was Adolf Hitler's deputy, Rudolf Hess, held in the Queen's House for four days in 1941.

WINDSOR CASTLE

CRESTING A CHALK CLIFF beside the Thames, Windsor Castle, founded about 1070, was one of nine strongholds built by William the Conqueror to encircle London; but by 1110 it had also become a royal residence in succession to an ancient Saxon palace at Old Windsor, three miles (five kilometres) downstream. For centuries, kings and queens lived in what are now the State Apartments along the northern escarpment of the Upper Ward, an imposing range remodelled over the years in turn by Edward III, Charles II and George IV, who also planned the present Private Apartments along the east and south ranges of the Quadrangle.

Windsor was somewhat neglected by George I and George II, but George III and Queen Charlotte liked this sturdy and impressive castle, with its Home Park, Great Park and outlying forest, and after a few visits they settled in 1778 in Queen's Lodge (now demolished) opposite the South Terrace, where they lived until they moved into the castle itself in 1804. The king chose a suite under the State Apartments in which to display his collection of books and pictures, while the queen elected to have her private rooms in the south-east tower and also, with her daughters, furnished elegant apartments on the east and south fronts.

During the reign of George IV, Sir Jeffry Wyatville added the Grand Corridor connecting the private suites, and created the present distinctive outline of crenellated towers. Wyatville's work included the heightening of the Round Tower, the stone keep standing massively in the Middle Ward on a mount cast up by local labour for William the Conqueror.

The glorious towers and turrets of Windsor Castle rise above the River Thames, dominated by the massive Round Tower, which was heightened in 1828–30. The magnificent view from the tower's battlemented walk embraces 12 counties.

ABOVE: *The King's Dining Room, dating from the reign of Charles II, is sumptuously decorated by Antonio Verrio with the foods of which banquets are made – fish, fowl and fruit. On the ceiling, the gods are seen enjoying this bounty.*

BELOW: *This amusing pineapple comport was part of a set of china made by Rockingham 1830–7. It was commissioned by William IV and is now on display in the castle's China Museum.*

George IV also completed the vista of Charles I's Long Walk with the equestrian statue of George III that stands on Snow Hill in the Great Park. This bronze colossus, popularly known as 'The Copper Horse', was designed as an affectionate filial tribute to the 'best of fathers' – George IV himself directed that the king's right hand should point toward the castle, his beloved home.

Today, Windsor is a royal palace and fortress under the direct control of the Sovereign, and is in constant use by Her Majesty The Queen, who uses it as a private retreat as well as the official Court residence at Easter and during Ascot Week.

St George's Chapel in the Lower Ward, built in 1475–1528, is the scene of the Garter Service held by Her Majesty each year on the Monday of Ascot Week. The Order of the Garter, the premier order of chivalry, was founded at Windsor by Edward III in 1348. In the chapel lie the sovereigns of Great Britain and their consorts from George III and Queen Charlotte onward – all but Queen Victoria and Prince Albert, who rest in their green-domed mausoleum at Frogmore in the Home Park Private, and Edward VIII, later Duke of Windsor, who was buried in 1972 in the royal cemetery adjoining the mausoleum. Earlier kings entombed in St George's Chapel include the 'Royal Martyr', Charles I. In 2002, Her Majesty Queen Elizabeth The Queen Mother was laid to rest in the chapel alongside her husband, George VI, and the ashes of her younger daughter, Princess Margaret, who pre-deceased her by just a few weeks.

RIGHT: *St George's Hall was created, in Gothic-revival style, during the reign of George IV by combining the original hall and chapel. The new ceiling seen here was installed during restoration work following the fire in 1992.*

BELOW: *The view down the Long Walk to the Norman Gate leading into the castle's Upper Ward. This glorious avenue, planted by Charles II in 1685, runs from the castle to the Great Park.*

FROGMORE HOUSE

A SECRET JEWEL IN THE CROWN of royal residences is Frogmore House. Queen Charlotte acquired this small mansion near Windsor Castle in 1792, and it became her favourite retreat. The architect James Wyatt converted the original house, built around 1680, for royal use, adding the existing colonnade and wings and giving the interior an elegant neoclassical feel. Restored in the 1980s, the house now reflects the various phases of its occupation. The grounds, originally laid out by Queen Charlotte and now within the private park of the castle, are occasionally opened to the public by permission of Her Majesty The Queen.

ABOVE: *The Mary Moser Room, Frogmore House. Mary Moser, a renowned flower painter, was commissioned by Queen Charlotte to create the illusion of an arbour open to the sky. The furniture mostly dates from Queen Charlotte's occupancy.*

The Great Fire of Windsor

On the night of 20 November 1992, fire broke out in The Queen's Private Chapel, spreading rapidly and gutting the Chapel, the State Dining Room and the Crimson Drawing Room. The ceilings of St George's Hall and the Grand Reception Room were also destroyed but, fortunately, very few treasures were lost. A huge programme of restoration work began immediately, and was completed in time for the 50th wedding anniversary of Her Majesty The Queen and Prince Philip, exactly five years later. Most of the rooms were restored to their original appearance, but the chapel was completely redesigned, and a new ceiling was created for St George's Hall.

SCOTTISH PALACES

Until the death of Queen Elizabeth I in 1603, Scotland was ruled by a separate kingship. The great Tudor line died with the queen, and her heir was James VI of Scotland, great-grandson of Henry VIII's sister, Margaret Tudor. He was crowned James I of England, and the kingdoms of England and Scotland were united.
The Scottish kings had built their own palaces and fortresses, and three of these – the Palace of Holyroodhouse, Linlithgow Palace and Falkland Palace – are still owned by the Sovereign.

THE PALACE OF HOLYROODHOUSE

A MILE EAST OF EDINBURGH CASTLE, backed by hills, stands the Palace of Holyroodhouse, originally the royal guest house of the now-ruined abbey of Holyrood, founded in 1128 by the Scottish king David I. James IV of Scotland built the existing north-west tower about 1501, and three years later brought to the palace his 13-year-old queen, Margaret Tudor. James IV was succeeded by his son, James V, and he in turn was succeeded by his daughter, Mary Queen of Scots.

To most people, Holyroodhouse is inexorably linked with the swift and violent murder here in March 1566 of David Rizzio, an Italian courtier who was known to be Mary's favourite. This dramatic incident – which, it is speculated, was instigated by her husband, Henry Stuart, Lord Darnley – took place in front of Mary when she was pregnant with the future James VI of Scotland.

RIGHT: *The King's Closet was one of the State Apartments built for Charles II after the Restoration in 1660. The room has a military theme, reflected in the ceiling decoration and in the carving framing the overmantel.*

Further building work had been carried out to the palace, although the west front was still unfinished, when on the night of 27 March 1603 Sir Robert Cary brought James VI the news that the English queen lay dead and that he was now also king of England.

James's grandson, Charles II, added the south-west tower, behind which he built the present State Apartments and Quadrangle; but neither he nor generations of his successors ever saw the finished palace. During the Jacobite Rebellion of 1745 the Young Pretender, Prince Charles Edward Stuart, reached Holyroodhouse and gave a ball in the Long Gallery, but after his defeat the palace lay deserted. The next British king to set foot on Scottish soil

A Macabre Fascination

When Queen Victoria first visited the Palace of Holyroodhouse in August 1850, she immediately asked to see the room in which David Rizzio had been murdered. Not realizing that she was in the presence of the queen and her daughters, the housekeeper obligingly showed them to the threshold of Queen Mary's bedchamber, embellishing the tale with vivid detail and pointing out the 'bloodstains' on the floor.

...as George IV, who visited Edinburgh in 1822 ...d held a levée at Holyroodhouse. The royal ...partments were occupied by Queen Victoria ...d Prince Albert in 1850 and, after 1911, when ...eorge V and Queen Mary made the first of ...eir state visits, the palace gradually came into ...e once more. Today, this beautiful and stately ...ifice is a fit setting for the Court which the ...esent Queen holds for a week each July.

LEFT: *'Boys Among Apple Trees', one of the Mortlake tapestries depicting playing boys that hang in the Queen's Ante-Chamber. This room, together with the Queen's Bed Chamber, originally formed James V's King's Apartment.*

11

LINLITHGOW PALACE

NOW IN PARTIAL RUIN, Linlithgow Palace was built from 1425 by James I on a promontory which almost divides Linlithgow Loch in two. The rooms of the quadrangular-shaped palace were furnished with tapestries and cloth of gold for the reception of James IV's bride, Margaret Tudor, but traditionally the young queen's favourite retreat was the little vaulted, octagonal turret chamber crowning the north-west tower, from which she watched and waited while her husband waged war against the English. He did not return – he was killed at the battle of Flodden in 1513.

His son, James V, also held court at Linlithgow, entertained by minstrels, actors and jesters. Here, on 8 December 1542, his second wife gave birth to the future Mary Queen of Scots. Mary's son, James VI, often stayed at Linlithgow before succeeding to the throne of England. Thirty years later, Charles I visited the palace, the last king to sleep at Linlithgow. In 1746, during the Jacobite Rebellion, troops commanded by the Duke of Cumberland stayed in the palace, kindling fires which they carelessly left burning. The flames spread and the palace was gutted, but its glory was not wholly destroyed, and in 1914 George V and Queen Mary held court in the roofless Great Hall.

FALKLAND PALACE

FALKLAND PALACE was built in the French Renaissance style by James IV and James V between 1501 and 1541, although remains of earlier buildings dating from the 12th century can still be seen in the grounds. The Stuart kings and queens stayed in the palace when hunting in the forest of Fife, and the troubled Mary Queen of Scots in particular loved its tranquillity. The east wing burnt down in 1654 when Cromwell's troops were stationed in the palace, but the south and east ranges are still intact and contain the Chapel Royal, the King's Bedchamber and the Queen's Room. In the gardens can be found the oldest royal tennis court in Britain, built in 1539.

Falkland Palace is managed for Her Majesty The Queen by The National Trust for Scotland.

ABOVE: *The romantic, partially ruined Linlithgow Palace sits on Linlithgow Loch and has been an inspiration both to poets and to artists, including Sir Walter Scott and J.M.W. Turner.*

LEFT: *The castle was built from 1425 by James I, whose arms are above the main entrance.*

ABOVE: *Falkland Palace, in Fife, was a favourite retreat of Stuart kings and queens, especially Mary Queen of Scots. Restoration work carried out by The National Trust for Scotland includes the King's Bedchamber and the Queen's Room in the East Range.*

HENRY VIII WAS WITHOUT DOUBT one of the most fascinating and colourful characters in British history. Although most notable for his determined quest to produce a son and heir to ensure continuity of the Tudor line, Henry was also known for his love of luxury and opulence – a passion that was reflected in the homes he created for himself, sometimes at the expense of others.

Downstream of the medieval royal Palace of Westminster stood York Place, built in the 13th century as the official London residence of the Archbishops of York. As such, it became the home in 1514 of Cardinal Thomas Wolsey, who 'most sumptuously and gloriously' enlarged the riverside mansion. Wolsey was a favourite of Henry VIII, but his failure to secure the king a divorce from Catherine of Aragon led to his being disgraced. On 22 October 1529 Wolsey yielded all his possessions to the king in a vain attempt to appease him. Within ten days Henry moved into York Place, which he renamed 'White Hall', and further enlarged the already palatial house. Whitehall Palace was to remain the seat of majesty in London for almost 200 years.

In 1619–22, the Banqueting House was built by Inigo Jones for James I. It stood beside the palace's main gate and was the first and most dominant Classical building in England. Its crowning glory is the ceiling, which was painted for Charles I by Sir Peter Paul Rubens to depict the apotheosis of James I and the triumphs of Stuart government; ironically, it was under this painted heaven that Charles walked to his death on 30 January 1649. The canvases for the ceiling arrived in England and were installed in 1635. After this, the king forbade the performance in the building of masques – which had been popularized by James I's queen, Anne of Denmark – to avoid damaging the ceiling with lamp-smoke.

After 1698, when most of Whitehall Palace was destroyed by fire caused by a laundress who left her linen too near the open flames in her airing-room, the Banqueting House became in turn a chapel and a museum. Its modern appearance dates from the early 19th century, when it was refaced; further restoration was carried out in 1973 to commemorate the 400th anniversary of the birth of Inigo Jones, and today it is still in use for state and society occasions.

BELOW: *The Banqueting House, all that remains of the great Whitehall Palace, still retains its classical-style exterior, although in the early 19th century the building was refaced and Georgian sash windows replaced the originals.*

ABOVE: *Queen Anne of Denmark, James I's consort depicted as a winged masquer. The queen often took part in masques – an early form of amateur theatre – designed by Inigo Jones with Ben Jonson and other poets.*

LEFT: *The simple but stunning elegance of the Banqueting House interior is seen to advantage here, beneath the ceiling painted by Rubens for Charles I to celebrate the triumphs of the Stuart government.*

BELOW: *A wall plaque commemorates the execution of Charles I in 1649.*

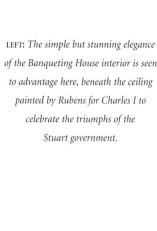

The Execution of Charles I

The Civil War was over, and the king sentenced to death; outside the Banqueting House, the scaffold stood in readiness. The king was to perish by his own front door. Charles I is believed to have stepped out on to the scaffold through a first-floor window, now no longer visible, over the entrance. Crowds huddling in the bitter cold on neighbouring rooftops marvelled at his courage and dignity as he knelt at the block and the executioner 'at one blow severed his head from his body'.

HAMPTON COURT PALACE

HAMPTON COURT PALACE, originally the huge and imposing country residence of the unfortunate Cardinal Thomas Wolsey, was, like his palace in London, to fall into the hands of Henry VIII.

An outline formed by red bricks in the paving of the palace's Clock Court shows where foundations of an earlier south front were revealed by excavations in 1965. The foundations were possibly those of the manor house of the Knights Hospitallers of St John of Jerusalem, from whom Wolsey acquired the estate in 1514. On this site, Wolsey not only created a palace of about 1,000 rooms – a place of 'extraordinary salubrity' – entered by the Great Gatehouse that leads from Outer Green Court on the west into Base Court and then into Clock Court, but also enclosed 1,800 acres (730 hectares) or so of land to form Hampton Court Park and Bushy Park.

Henry VIII had a very hearty appetite for rich food, and when he took possession of the palace in 1529, one of his first tasks was to extend the kitchens; today, the restored Tudor kitchens are one of the palace's most fascinating attractions. Henry's vast household of 1,200 were served their meals in the magnificent Great Hall, which was also the striking entrance to Henry's new state apartments, built around a third courtyard. The Great Watching Chamber was the first of these apartments; although modernized, this room still retains its original decorated ceiling and magnificent tapestries.

ABOVE: *Henry VIII's Great Hall, the largest room in the pala* *The gloriously ornate hammerbeam roof and the Flemish* *tapestries date from Henry's reign; the carved stags' heads* *and the stained glass were added later.*

BELOW: *The West Front, showing the gatehouse built by Wols* *Above the gate are the arms of Henry VIII, and the moat* *bridge is flanked with the King's Beasts. The wings to* *either side housed Henry's vast kitchens.*

ABOVE: *The timber vaulted ceiling, with carved and gilded pendants from 1556, is the crowning glory of the Chapel Royal. The oak reredos was carved in the 18th century by the master carver Grinling Gibbons.*

Henry VIII was, of course, famous for his six wives, and there is evidence of their presence around the palace. Below the Astronomical Clock, for example, is Anne Boleyn's Gateway; Henry and Jane Seymour were betrothed at Hampton Court, and Jane died here shortly after giving birth to their son and heir, Prince Edward, who was baptized in the Chapel Royal; and it is said that the ghost of Henry's fifth wife, Catherine Howard, who was imprisoned at Hampton Court before being sent to her execution for high treason at the Tower of London in 1542, still shrieks with terror in the Haunted Gallery.

Henry worked off his excesses playing tennis and bowls in the grounds, and hunting in the vast park. He built the first tennis court at Hampton Court in about 1530, and although various improvements were made during the 17th century to Henry's original court, it is still the oldest court in use in the world today.

LEFT: The allegorical decoration on the spectacular King's Staircase, painted by Antonio Verrio, represents William III's triumph in deposing the Stuart king James II. The wrought-iron balustrade was designed by Jean Tijou.

Most of Henry VIII's royal apartments were destroyed when Sir Christopher Wren created the present Fountain Court, around which he built for William III the extensive King's Apartments. For Mary II, Wren began to create the Queen's State Apartments, but Mary died before the work was completed; Queen Anne then commissioned further work before her own death in 1714. The apartments were eventually completed by the future George II and Queen Caroline, and George was the last sovereign to live at Hampton Court.

In 1986 the King's Apartments were badly damaged when fire broke out and today the meticulously restored rooms are displayed as they were in the reign of William III. Hampton Court Palace survives as a magnificent memorial of majesty.

RIGHT: A view of the South Front, showing the newly restored Privy Garden. The South Front houses the King's Apartments, which were restored following severe fire damage in 1986.

Hampton Court Palace Gardens

The famous gardens at Hampton Court Palace were originally laid out by Henry VIII, but were remodelled by William III and Mary II, who shared a passion for gardening. The Privy Garden has been restored and planted with the same varieties used when it was completed for William in 1702. Also surviving from this date is the Maze, almost half a mile (0.8 kilometres) of paths running in a deceptively complex pattern through tall clipped hedges. The Lower Orangery, now a picture gallery, was specially built to house Queen Mary's collection of botanical specimens gathered from the Canary Islands and Virginia. Nearby is the Great Vine, planted in 1768 by 'Capability' Brown and still producing a generous yield of grapes each year.

The wonderful gardens are the setting for the annual Hampton Court Flower Show, where imaginative traditional and contemporary garden layouts and exciting new varieties of plants inspire thousands of enthusiastic gardeners.

ABOVE: A medallion portrait of the Prince of Wales, the future George II, on the ceiling of the Queen's State Bedchamber. He was the last king to live at Hampton Court, making his final visit in 1737.

ST JAMES'S PALACE

THE HOSPITAL OF ST JAMES IN THE FIELDS, a sanatorium for female lepers, occupied the site where St James's Palace now stands before it was acquired by Henry VIII in 1532. St James's, along with Whitehall Palace, originally formed part of the Palace of Westminster. Henry's turreted gatehouse, the entrance to the palace, still stands on the North Front beside the Chapel Royal, leading into Colour Court, the former Great Court.

Only a few original features remain of the South Front, where the royal apartments were built around what is now Friary Court, with gates opening into St James's Park; but the present principal State Rooms, overlooking the Mall, have a Tudor-style exterior. Two of the rooms, at the west end, were added by Sir Christopher Wren for James II and used as the Great Drawing Room and Great Council Chamber; when Whitehall Palace burned down and St James's became the principal royal residence, these rooms formed part of the sovereign's state suite.

The south and east ranges of Friary Court were in turn destroyed by fire in 1809, and today Marlborough Road cuts through the site, dividing from the rest of the palace the Queen's Chapel, designed by Inigo Jones for Charles I's Roman Catholic consort, Queen Henrietta Maria.

In 1827 the Queen Anne Room was built on the South Front as the approach from the Grand Staircase to Wren's State Rooms, which became the Entrée Room and the Throne Room.

Today, the Throne Room, sumptuously decorated in white, gold and crimson, is often used as a venue for official functions; here, the Lord Mayor and Councillors of the City of Westminster present their address of welcome to visiting Heads of State. St James's is also home to several members of the Royal Family, and is a busy working palace housing the offices of The Prince of Wales and various Royal Household departments.

RIGHT: *The Tudor gatehouse of St James Palace. Little remains of Henry VIII's palace, which was virtually destroyed by fire in 1809, although the principal State Rooms, overlooking the Mall, have a Tudor-style exterior.*

BELOW: *The palace's Tapestry Room was redecorated in distinctive style in 1866 by William Morris, the eminent Victorian designer and craftsman.*

BELOW: *The Entrée Room, one of the State Rooms built for James II by Sir Christopher Wren on the South Front.*

Lost in the Corridors of Power

The old Tudor palace was a confusing maze of passages, backstairs, court suites and domestic offices enclosing seven courtyards. George III scornfully referred to it as 'that dust-trap', and his wife's keeper of the robes, Fanny Burney, recorded in her journal how she completely lost her way during a state occasion and was only discovered after making a long and frenzied appeal for help.

THE QUEEN'S HOUSE, GREENWICH

WHEN JAMES VI OF SCOTLAND also became James I of England, he moved his household to London, bringing with him his consort, Anne of Denmark. In 1614 James gave Anne the Manor of Greenwich, where she commissioned Inigo Jones to build a new house on the site of the garden gatehouse of Placentia, the Tudor palace which had been the birthplace of both Henry VIII and his daughter, Elizabeth I.

Studying Andrea Palladio's architecture in Italy, Jones had seen a villa at Poggio a Caiano, remodelled by Guiliano da Sangallo and owned by Lorenzo de Medici. This villa undoubtedly influenced his design for the Queen's House, one of his most notable innovations in the classical style. Work on the house was begun in 1616, but stopped when Anne became ill in 1618, and only resumed in 1629 when Charles I gave Greenwich to his queen, Henrietta Maria.

The house was built in an 'H'-shape astride the Deptford to Woolwich road, with the Queen's

Apartments on the north side connected by a central 'bridge' to the King's Apartments and Loggia, which overlooked the park on the south.

The exterior was completed in 1635, and leading European painters were commissioned to decorate the interior with ceiling panels and other art works. The elegant rooms were adorned with classical sculpture from Charles I's collection. Today, the ceiling of the galleried Hall, which rises through two storeys and forms a perfect cube, has modern copies of the panels, originally painted by Gentileschi of Pisa, depicting the Arts of Peace; the originals are in Marlborough House, next to St James's Palace.

The Queen's House lost its treasures during the Civil War, but was refitted at the Restoration by Charles II, who built two more 'bridge' rooms, creating a square shape on the first floor. The colonnades and two flanking wings were added in the early 19th century to provide extra accommodation when the house was used as the Royal Hospital School. In 1934, after the school moved to Suffolk, the buildings were taken over by the National Maritime Museum, and until recently the Queen's House held some of the museum's exhibits. In the late 20th century, the house was restored and part of it now echoes the late 17th-century royal residence.

BELOW: *The King's Presence Chamber was designed by Inigo Jones for Charles I's queen, Henrietta Maria. The vivid blue colour is based on the original smalt, a pigment made from crushed glass coloured with oxide of cobalt.*

ABOVE: *This vista of the Queen's House in Greenwich shows the house flanked the twin galleries of the National Maritime Museum, with the Old Royal Observatory on the hill in the distance*

The House of Delight

A glorious vista of the Queen's House and the former Royal Naval College, with the Queen's House as the centrepiece and the heights of Greenwich Park rising beyond it to the Old Royal Observatory, can be seen from the Island Gardens of the Isle of Dogs, on the opposite bank of the Thames.

LEFT: *This model of a royal yacht, dating from about 1670, reflects both the maritime tradition connected with the Queen's House and its former role as a sovereign's residence.*

23

KENSINGTON PALACE

LEFT: *The serene South Front of Kensington Palace, designed for William III and Mary II as part of the transformation of the house from a modest suburban mansion to a home fit for a king and queen.*

RIGHT: *Queen Victoria's Bedchamber where the young princess was asleep when news came of her accession to the throne. Many of the paintings were Christmas or birthday gifts exchanged between the queen and her consort, Prince Albert.*

IN 1688, JAMES II WAS EXILED and William of Orange was invited to rule Britain jointly with his wife, James's daughter Mary. William III and Mary II came to England, exchanging their pleasant Dutch palaces for Whitehall, where the un-embanked Thames frequently flooded the cellars and the river mists aggravated William's asthma. Hampton Court Palace offered a welcome alternative, but a London residence was essential.

The following year, William purchased Nottingham House, a modest suburban mansion, soon to be renamed Kensington House and later Kensington Palace. The house was ideal, being agreeably situated on rising ground in its own gardens west of Hyde Park, but was too small for the royal household. However, Sir Christopher Wren enlarged it so competently that five months later the king's birthday ball was held there, followed by the royal Christmas celebrations.

In 1690–1, Mary added the Queen's Staircase leading to the Queen's Gallery; the King's Gallery, uniting the King's Staircase and King's Bedchamber, forms part of the South Front built in 1695. The charming Orangery was added in 1704, during the reign of Queen Anne. After the accession of the House of Hanover in 1714, the three principal State Rooms – the Privy Chamber, the Cupola Room and the King's Drawing Room – were built for George I and decorated by the architect and designer William Kent.

George II, who was very fond of Kensington Palace, died there suddenly on the morning of 25 October 1760, leaving his unquiet ghost to haunt the courtyards and terrify the sentries on night duty. His wife, Queen Caroline, a keen gardener, transformed the grounds of the palace into the lovely gardens seen today.

George III deserted the palace in favour of Buckingham House, but his granddaughter, Princess Victoria of Kent, was born here on 24 May 1819. The palace was very briefly used as a sovereign's residence when Victoria became queen on 20 June 1837; three weeks later she drove in state to take up residence at Buckingham Palace.

BELOW: *The Sunken Garden, modelled the Tudor Garden at Hampton Court was created during Edward VII's reign. The lead fountains were originally cisterns in the palace – a commendable example of recycling!*

Princess Mary of Teck, the future queen
nsort of George V, was born at Kensington on
May 1867, and her lasting interest in the happy
me of her childhood inspired the preservation
the Victorian style of the private rooms used by
r and her mother, a charming contrast to the
jesty of the State Rooms.

Today, Kensington continues its long history as
esidence for members of the Royal Family. The
st-known residents in recent years were Diana,
ncess of Wales and Princess Margaret.

All the King's Men

William Kent's paintings on the walls of the King's Staircase depict a
fascinating collection of court personalities, including George I's Turkish
body-servants, Mustapha and Mehemet, captured as boys in the Turkish
wars, his Polish page, Ulric, and Peter the Wild Boy, a human misfit found
in the Hanoverian woods in 1725 and brought by the king to England,
where he survived on a royal pension until 1785.

KEW PALACE

ABOVE: *The pretty, 'doll's-house' exterior of Kew Palace. The brickwork has been restored with a special wash to blend the mortar into the bricks, giving the house an identical appearance to when it was first built.*

KEW PALACE, ALSO KNOWN AS 'The Dutch House', was built in *c.*1631 by Samuel Fortrey, a Dutch merchant, over the vaults of a Tudor house. The palace is the sole survivor of a succession of palaces at Richmond on the River Thames, and was only briefly inhabited by a sovereign, although it was used by the royal family from 1729–1818.

The Dutch House which stood opposite the White House at Kew Green, was leased as a royal annexe to Queen Caroline when she and George lived in Richmond Lodge, formerly the keeper's lodge in the old royal deer park. Augusta, Prince of Wales, Queen Caroline's daughter-in-law, use the annexe as a nursery, and George III lived he as a boy. He succeeded to the throne in 1760, and on his marriage Richmond Lodge was settle on his consort, Queen Charlotte, as part of her dower. The king and queen continued to make

RIGHT: *The Queen's Garden, a tranquil place for quiet contemplation tucked away behind Kew Palace.*

The Royal Botanic Gardens

The Royal Botanic Gardens at Kew were created in 1841.
The west part was formed from the gardens laid out by
Queen Caroline when she lived at Richmond Lodge, while the
east section took in the grounds of the White House at
Kew Green, where Queen Caroline's daughter-in-law,
Augusta, Dowager Princess of Wales, founded the original
'botanick garden' in 1759. The grounds of Kew Palace were
added to the gardens in the early 20th century.
Today, the world-famous gardens, dotted with a
number of fascinating listed buildings and 'special interest'
areas, have the largest collection of living plants.

BELOW: *Queen Charlotte's cottage, a fairy-tale thatched tea-house
originally built about 1770, stands at the south-west corner of the Royal
Botanic Gardens. The Royal Family often took tea in this room.*

the royal summer residence, and enjoyed the environment so much that the king planned to build an imposing new riverside lace. The plan was to remain just a dream, however, and in 1772 orge and Queen Charlotte moved to the White House, where his dowed mother had lived until her death, leaving Richmond dge to be demolished.

At that time, the White House and its grounds were not royal operty but held on lease. The king and queen changed its name to ew House', and later it was officially referred to as 'The Palace'. e Dutch House was used as the boyhood home of the future ng George IV and his brother, Frederick, Duke of York, and in 82 it was bought for Queen Charlotte.

In 1801, the king and queen moved into the Dutch House while gotiating the purchase of the White House estate. Although the g planned and built a new palace nearby, they continued to visit e Dutch House, and indeed Queen Charlotte died here in 1818 eorge's last visit was in 1806). The White House had meanwhile en demolished, and the Dutch House was condemned to follow, t George IV gave it a reprieve and eventually it became known as w Palace. In 1899 Queen Victoria, granddaughter of George III d Queen Charlotte, opened it to the public.

THE ROYAL PAVILION, BRIGHTON

THE ROYAL PAVILION IN BRIGHTON is a testament to the flamboyant taste of George IV in his earlier years as Prince of Wales. Brighton was a fishing village until the 18th century, when physicians began to proclaim the curative powers of sea-bathing. In 1783, soon after his coming of age, the prince stayed here and liked it so much that he invited Henry Holland to build an elegant classical villa for him, boosting the town's social prestige.

Holland's house, the original Pavilion, was never totally remodelled, but in 1815–22 the renowned architect John Nash transformed it into a unique 'palace', a fantasy of Indian domes, pinnacles and minarets. The Entrance Hall and Long Gallery, the Great Kitchen, the Banqueting (or Dragon) Room and the Music Room date from the same period. Chinese interiors had long been a feature of the Pavilion and the theme reaches its utmost brilliance in the Chinese landscapes and water-lily chandeliers of the Music Room, and the great gold and silver dragons and palm-tree ceiling of the Banqueting Room.

ABOVE: *The fantastic domes, pinnacl and minarets of the Royal Pavilion, b by John Nash for the flamboyant George IV, appear almost unreal an could be mistaken for the work of a master confectioner.*

LEFT: *The dramatic Banqueting Roo is one of the most magnificent rooms the pavilion. The decorations were created by artist-designer Robert Jon and include an enormous palm tre in the domed ceiling.*

Queen Victoria and Prince Albert launched their scarlet and gold
...gh from the Pavilion in the snow of February 1845, but although
...queen liked 'this strange building' she found Brighton too public,
...d that summer she and the prince moved to their own seaside
...me, Osborne House on the Isle of Wight.

...Restoration work to both the interior and exterior of the Pavilion,
...ether with the return of many of the original furnishings from
...ckingham Palace, has ensured that this delicious architectural
...fection is preserved, a unique memorial of the Regency age.

A Trio of Houses

The Royal Pavilion was one of three homes created by
George IV when he was Prince of Wales. The other two were
Carlton House in London and the Royal Lodge in Windsor
Great Park, a thatched 'cottage' built by John Nash when the
...rince became Regent in 1811. Carlton House was demolished
...after George's accession in 1820, while the Royal Lodge, now
almost entirely rebuilt, survives as a private royal home.

ABOVE: *The elaborate chandelier in the Banqueting Room
is suspended from the claws of a huge silver dragon.*

BUCKINGHAM HOUSE WAS ORIGINALLY BUILT for John Sheffield, Duke of Buckingham, early in the 18th century. The mansion was described as 'a graceful palace … not to be contemned by the greatest monarch', and indeed the Prince and Princess of Wales, later to become George II and Queen Caroline, were anxious to obtain it when Buckingham died. His widow refused to part with the house, however, and it stayed in the family until 1762 when Buckingham's son, Sir Charles Sheffield, sold it for £28,000 to George III.

King George and his new bride and consort, Queen Charlotte, were very happy in their new home, planning 'Sumptuous and Stately Improvements' and taking the air in an idyllic setting of lawns and lime avenues and a meadow full of cattle. The queen returned to their former home, St James's Palace, for the birth of their first child, George, Prince of Wales, later George IV, but the rest of their 15 children were born at Buckingham House, which became known as the Queen's House or the Queen's Palace. In 1809 some of the royal apartments at St James's were destroyed by fire, and many social ceremonies were transferred to the Queen's House.

When George IV acceded to the throne in 1820, he instructed John Nash to remodel his childhood home. Nash retained the skeleton of the original house but extended the garden side to provide the king with a sequence of new State Rooms opening out of the Picture Gallery. The Royal Closet, White Drawing Room, Music Room, Blue Drawing Room and State Dining Room overlooked the garden to the west, while to the east of the Picture Gallery were the Throne Room, the Green Drawing Room over the Grand Entrance, and the Guard Chamber. Nash's Grand Staircase leads up in flights marble steps from the Grand Hall, which has along its west side the Marble Hall and Semi-State Rooms opening on to the terrace.

Out of Bounds

Planning restrictions were unheard of in the 18th century. To obtain the perfect site for his new mansion, the Duke of Buckingham not only trespassed on the Mulberry Garden, which belonged to the Crown, but also lopped off a piece of St James's Park and diverted the road.

ABOVE: *The white marble Grand Staircase rises out of the Grand Hall and leads in a graceful sweep to the State Rooms on the first floor. The gilt bronze balustrade is the finest example of its type in England.*

ABOVE: *The East Front of Buckingham Palace is one of the most famous façades in the world. The balcony in the central portico has been the scene of countless memorable appearances by the Royal Family.*

RIGHT: *The Picture Gallery runs between the main State Rooms and is lit through the glazed arched ceiling. Besides the delectable collection of paintings in the gallery, objets d'art in porcelain and lacquer are also on display.*

Buckingham Palace was still unfinished when Queen Victoria came to the throne in 1837, and she was the first sovereign to live here. To accommodate Victoria's large family, Edward Blore added the East Front in 1847–53; it was remodelled in Portland stone by Sir Aston Webb almost 70 years later.

Today, Buckingham Palace is more than just a royal residence – it is the symbolic heart of the constitutional monarchy. The sumptuous rooms, furnished with countless beautiful treasures, set a spectacular scene for the royal ceremonies, banquets, receptions and investitures hosted by Her Majesty The Queen and her family.

RIGHT: The Blue Drawing Room overlooks the beautiful palace gardens, and is one of the finest rooms in the palace. Guests of Her Majesty The Queen and her family gather here on great state and diplomatic occasions.

BELOW: An intricately chased silver gilt ewer and stand, one of a pair made for George IV in 1822 by Rundell, Bridge & Rundell.